April 22, 2000

Happy 4th Bir...
Love You...
Grandpa & Grandma J.

EL DORADO COUNTY LIBRARY

3 1738 00875 2725

DISCARD

D0130884

EL DORADO COUNTY LIBRARY
345 FAIR LANE
PLACERVILLE, CA 95667

DISCARD

Copyright © 1993, 1999 Kidsbooks Inc. and Tony Tallarico
3535 West Peterson Ave.
Chicago, IL 60659

All rights reserved including the right
of reproduction in whole or in part in any form.

Manufactured in the United States of America

Visit us at www.kidsbooks.com
Volume discounts available for group purchases.

WHERE ARE THEY?

DETECT DONALD

It was a dark and rainy night in Hollywood. Detective Donald had stopped to eat at his favorite diner.

DETECT DONALD AT THE CHEEZ-E DINER AND...

- ☐ Arrow
- ☐ Bat
- ☐ Bird
- ☐ Bow ties (3)
- ☐ Bowling ball
- ☐ Cactus
- ☐ Convict
- ☐ Cook
- ☐ Crown
- ☐ Dracula
- ☐ Dragon
- ☐ Eyeglasses (3)
- ☐ Fish
- ☐ Genie
- ☐ Ghost
- ☐ Guitar
- ☐ Heart
- ☐ Humpty Dumpty
- ☐ Jack-o'-lantern
- ☐ Mouse
- ☐ Pirate
- ☐ Rabbit
- ☐ Skull
- ☐ Stars (3)
- ☐ Super heroes
- ☐ Top hat
- ☐ Two-headed man
- ☐ Waitresses (2)
- ☐ Witch
- ☐ Wristwatch

When he stepped outside, he detected something strange going on. First he saw a large group of strange characters. Then....

...Detective Donald almost got run over by a horse and carriage! There were no cars or buses and people were wearing wigs and funny hats. Detective Donald thought he saw George Washington—but it couldn't be! He decided to investigate to find out what was going on.

DETECT DONALD IN COLONIAL AMERICA AND...

- ☐ Antenna
- ☐ Baseball
- ☐ Basket
- ☐ Bell
- ☐ Ben Franklin
- ☐ Betsy Ross
- ☐ Bone
- ☐ Broom
- ☐ Bucket
- ☐ Candles (2)
- ☐ Cannonballs (4)
- ☐ Cats (2)
- ☐ Chicken
- ☐ Clock
- ☐ Dogs (2)
- ☐ Drums (3)
- ☐ Duck
- ☐ Ear of corn
- ☐ Flower vase
- ☐ Horses (4)
- ☐ Kites (2)
- ☐ Lamppost
- ☐ Mouse
- ☐ One dollar bill
- ☐ Saw
- ☐ Shopping bag
- ☐ Spinning wheel
- ☐ TV set
- ☐ Wagons (2)
- ☐ Watering can

Suddenly, two knights on horseback carrying long lances went charging by. A king, queen, knights and maidens were watching a jousting tournament. *Where was he now?* wondered Detective Donald.

DETECT DONALD IN THE MIDDLE AGES AND...

☐ Alligator
☐ Balloons (2)
☐ Birds (2)
☐ Candy cane
☐ Dog
☐ Doorbell
☐ Fan
☐ Fish
☐ Hot dog
☐ Ice-cream cone
☐ Jack-o'-lantern
☐ Jester
☐ King
☐ Kite
☐ Musician
☐ Periscope
☐ Pig
☐ Pot
☐ Robin Hood
☐ Rose
☐ Santa Claus
☐ Skull
☐ Sock
☐ Stars (2)
☐ Target
☐ Toast
☐ Umpire
☐ Unicorn
☐ Vendor
☐ Wizard

After watching the tournament for awhile, Detective Donald walked through the castle...

...and into a room filled with laughter! There were lots of cartoon characters acting silly all around him. Things were getting stranger and stranger.

DETECT DONALD IN CARTOONLAND AND...

- ☐ Balloon
- ☐ Banana peel
- ☐ Baseball
- ☐ Beehive
- ☐ Book
- ☐ Brush
- ☐ Cars (2)
- ☐ Cheese
- ☐ Clothesline
- ☐ Fire hydrant
- ☐ Fish (2)
- ☐ Fishing pole
- ☐ Flower
- ☐ Ghost
- ☐ Golf club
- ☐ Hose
- ☐ Ice-cream cone
- ☐ Magnifying glass
- ☐ Net
- ☐ Owl
- ☐ Sandwich
- ☐ Soap
- ☐ Star
- ☐ Sunglasses (2)
- ☐ Super dude
- ☐ Train engine
- ☐ Turtle
- ☐ TV set
- ☐ Umbrella

As Detective Donald walked through a hole in the wall, he heard...

...“Ahoy mates, a landlubber!” It was a pirate ship, and pirates were dashing about with swords doing battle with anyone and everyone.

DETECT DONALD AT THE PIRATES' BATTLE AND...

- ☐ Basketball
- ☐ Birds (3)
- ☐ Broom
- ☐ Candle
- ☐ Cannonballs (4)
- ☐ Captain Hook
- ☐ Cat
- ☐ Cup
- ☐ Duck
- ☐ Fish
- ☐ Football
- ☐ Guitar
- ☐ Half moon
- ☐ Headless horseman
- ☐ Hearts (2)
- ☐ Hot dog
- ☐ Jack-o'-lantern
- ☐ Knight
- ☐ Mice (7)
- ☐ Mirror
- ☐ Piano
- ☐ Rooster
- ☐ Sailboat
- ☐ Snake
- ☐ Top hat
- ☐ Treasure chest
- ☐ Turtles (3)
- ☐ Watering can
- ☐ Wooden legs (3)
- ☐ Yellow brick road

Detective Donald thought it best to quickly move on.

What was happening?
Detective Donald's
surroundings began to
change before his very
eyes! Strange buildings
and bizarre creatures
replaced the pirates.

DETECT DONALD IN THE WORLD OF THE FUTURE AND...

- ☐ Baby carriage
- ☐ Bat
- ☐ Bottle
- ☐ Bow
- ☐ Clothespin
- ☐ Dog
- ☐ Flat tire
- ☐ Hammer
- ☐ Key
- ☐ Kite
- ☐ Ladder
- ☐ Little red riding creature
- ☐ Mailbox
- ☐ Parachute
- ☐ Pencil
- ☐ Phonograph record
- ☐ Pocket watch
- ☐ Red wagon
- ☐ Submarine sandwich
- ☐ Schoolbag
- ☐ Sled
- ☐ Snowman
- ☐ Straw
- ☐ Teeth
- ☐ Tree
- ☐ Two-headed creature
- ☐ Tepee
- ☐ Vacuum cleaner
- ☐ Witch

Out an exit he went,
and into...

...French history a few hundred years ago. He was more confused than ever. Maybe I'm just having a weird dream, he thought.

DETECT DONALD IN NAPOLEON'S FRANCE AND...

- ☐ Alligator
- ☐ Axe
- ☐ Ballerina
- ☐ Balloon
- ☐ Baker
- ☐ Bell
- ☐ Cake
- ☐ Cannon
- ☐ Dracula
- ☐ Dragon
- ☐ Duck
- ☐ Eight ball
- ☐ Firecracker
- ☐ Flower
- ☐ French poodle
- ☐ King Kong
- ☐ Medals (2)
- ☐ Mermaid
- ☐ Movie camera
- ☐ Mummy
- ☐ Old tire
- ☐ One-eyed alien
- ☐ Pinocchio
- ☐ Radio
- ☐ Rapunzel
- ☐ Sailor
- ☐ Scarecrow
- ☐ Shark
- ☐ Tarzan
- ☐ Unicorn

Detective Donald kept searching and searching for clues. Next he found himself...

...in an army camp during basic training. Some soldiers were having fun, but most were happy when training was over. Detective Donald noticed a movie camera. Hmmm, he wondered, haven't I seen one somewhere before?

DETECT DONALD AT FORT KNOCKS AND...

- ☐ Ape
- ☐ Bat
- ☐ Bird
- ☐ Bodiless ghost
- ☐ Bombs (2)
- ☐ Cactus
- ☐ Chimneys (2)
- ☐ Cook
- ☐ Dunce cap
- ☐ Fan
- ☐ Fish (2)
- ☐ Jack-o'-lantern
- ☐ Lemonade stand
- ☐ Kite
- ☐ Medal
- ☐ Oil can
- ☐ Periscope
- ☐ Pitcher
- ☐ Pot
- ☐ Rat
- ☐ Robin Hood
- ☐ Sergeant's stripes (5)
- ☐ Skulls (2)
- ☐ Slingshot
- ☐ Snake
- ☐ Sock
- ☐ Traffic ticket
- ☐ Turtle
- ☐ Volcano

Donald walked past the chow line and into...

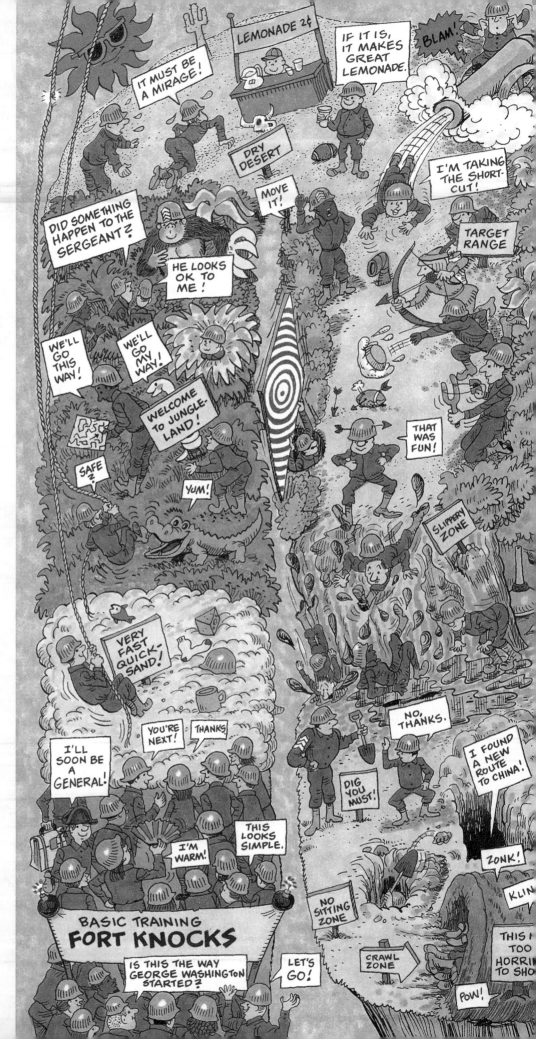

...the Roman Coliseum. But it wasn't a ruin! It was full of ancient Romans rooting for or against gladiators.

DETECT DONALD IN ANCIENT ROME AND...

- ☐ Abraham Lincoln
- ☐ Banana peel
- ☐ Bones (2)
- ☐ Boots
- ☐ Cheerleader
- ☐ Cleopatra
- ☐ Dog
- ☐ Dragons (2)
- ☐ Electric fan
- ☐ Elephant
- ☐ Football
- ☐ Giraffe
- ☐ Guitar
- ☐ Hot dog
- ☐ Hourglass
- ☐ Jester
- ☐ Kite
- ☐ Lions (3)
- ☐ Lunch boxes (2)
- ☐ Necktie
- ☐ Net
- ☐ Pig
- ☐ Raindrops (2)
- ☐ Red scarf
- ☐ Secret door
- ☐ Soccer ball
- ☐ Spears (2)
- ☐ Tin man
- ☐ Vendors (2)
- ☐ Watch
- ☐ Watering can

Detective Donald ducked out behind the big wooden horse and immediately ran into...

...a wooly mammoth! It was huge and hairy, but how did it get here? Or, how did *he* get *there*? The spear-carrying cave people frightened Detective Donald so he leapt out of their way.

DETECT DONALD IN PREHISTORIC TIMES AND...

- ☐ Ape
- ☐ Arrow
- ☐ Baby bird
- ☐ Basketball
- ☐ Bicycle
- ☐ Bone
- ☐ Book
- ☐ Burglar
- ☐ Cannon
- ☐ Chef
- ☐ Clipboard
- ☐ Helmet
- ☐ Juggler
- ☐ Kettle
- ☐ Mailbox
- ☐ Nets (2)
- ☐ Periscope
- ☐ Pole-vaulter
- ☐ Rabbit
- ☐ Rocket
- ☐ Rocking chair
- ☐ Rocking horse
- ☐ Roller skates
- ☐ Skateboard
- ☐ Skier
- ☐ Tennis racket
- ☐ Toothbrush
- ☐ Tuba
- ☐ Turtle
- ☐ Umbrella
- ☐ Witch

Donald continued on until he came to the back of a curtain. He opened it in time to hear...

...“And now...” He was standing on a stage receiving an award! But why? Then a very embarrassed Detective Donald realized that, without knowing it, he had just walked through ten movie sets!

DETECT DONALD AT THE ACADEMY AWARDS AND...

- ☐ Aliens (2)
- ☐ Arrows (2)
- ☐ Baseball cap
- ☐ Bird
- ☐ "Boo" (2)
- ☐ Bowling ball
- ☐ Broken heart
- ☐ Candle
- ☐ Cook
- ☐ Darts (5)
- ☐ Dog
- ☐ Elephant
- ☐ Envelope
- ☐ Fish
- ☐ Flower
- ☐ Fork
- ☐ Ghost
- ☐ Half moon
- ☐ Heart
- ☐ Ice skates
- ☐ Lens cap
- ☐ Masks (2)
- ☐ Microphone
- ☐ Mushroom
- ☐ Pencil
- ☐ Rabbit
- ☐ Scarf
- ☐ Skulls (2)
- ☐ Snake
- ☐ Tomahawk

WHERE ARE THEY?

FIND FRANKIE

It is the night of the Monster Club meeting. Every monster member, young and old, ugly and uglier is in attendance. The clubhouse is to be torn down and the monsters need a new place to meet. All the monsters are listening carefully—except Frankie.

FIND FRANKIE AT THE MONSTER CLUB MEETING AND...

☐ Arrow
☐ Ax
☐ Balloon
☐ Bats (4)
☐ Birdcage
☐ Bones (4)
☐ Broom
☐ Candles (7)
☐ Candy canes (2)
☐ Clothesline
☐ Cobweb
☐ Coffins (2)
☐ Cup
☐ Grapes
☐ Hot dog
☐ Jack-o'-lantern
☐ Mice (3)
☐ Nail
☐ Noose
☐ Pie
☐ Rabbit
☐ Skulls (4)
☐ Teddy bear
☐ TV set
☐ Voodoo doll
☐ Yo-yo

Suddenly...

...Frankie is lost in the outside world! There are so many sights and sounds, and so much to see. Maybe he can find a new meeting place for the monsters.

FIND FRANKIE ON THE STREET AND...

☐ Alien
☐ Bird singing
☐ Bowling ball
☐ Cat
☐ Elephant
☐ Falling flowerpot
☐ Fire hydrants (3)
☐ Flower van
☐ Football
☐ Guitar
☐ Hamburger
☐ Humpty Dumpty
☐ Karate bird
☐ King
☐ Kite
☐ Monkey
☐ Moose
☐ Mummy
☐ Ostrich
☐ Pizza
☐ Pogo stick
☐ Quicksand
☐ Rocket
☐ Santa Claus
☐ Scarecrow
☐ Tennis player
☐ Toothbrush
☐ Tuba
☐ Turtle
☐ Viking
☐ Water-skier

Frankie wonders where he should go first.

Wow! There's a lot going on in this store! Frankie can easily get lost in this dizzy, busy place.

FIND FRANKIE IN THE SUPER SUPERMARKET AND...

- ☐ Banana peel
- ☐ Basketball
- ☐ Bird
- ☐ Boat
- ☐ Bone
- ☐ Cactus
- ☐ Candles (2)
- ☐ Carrots
- ☐ Cheerleader
- ☐ Clown
- ☐ Duck
- ☐ Elephant
- ☐ "Fido"
- ☐ Fish heads
- ☐ Hammock
- ☐ Igloo
- ☐ Jack-o'-lantern
- ☐ Marshmallow
- ☐ Mermaid
- ☐ Mouse
- ☐ Periscope
- ☐ Ping-Pong ball
- ☐ Roller skates
- ☐ Six other monsters
- ☐ Skull
- ☐ Snowman
- ☐ Surfer
- ☐ Thief
- ☐ Tin Man
- ☐ Toast
- ☐ Wagon
- ☐ Witch
- ☐ Yo-yo

After all this activity, Frankie needs to find a quiet, dark place to relax.

Unfortunately, this show is so bad that even a nice monster like Frankie can't watch it for long.

FIND FRANKIE
AT THE THEATER
AND...

☐ Alligator
☐ Arrows (2)
☐ Camel
☐ Candle
☐ Chicken
☐ Clipboard
☐ Cowboy
☐ Deer
☐ Elephants (3)
☐ Fire hydrant
☐ Fish (4)
☐ Frog
☐ Ghosts (3)
☐ Giraffe
☐ Hammer
☐ Jack-in-the-box
☐ Jack-o'-lantern
☐ Lost shoe
☐ Mice (3)
☐ Octopus
☐ Paintbrush
☐ Peter Pan
☐ Pillow
☐ Satellite dish
☐ Snail
☐ Star
☐ Tin Man
☐ TV set
☐ Umbrellas (2)

Frankie needs some fresh air. So it's off to...

...a place where the creatures look even stranger than he does. Some have fur and some have feathers. Some have horns. Some are scary!

FIND FRANKIE AT THE ZOO AND...

☐ Baby taking a bath
☐ Balloons (6)
☐ Beach balls (3)
☐ Books (2)
☐ Brooms (2)
☐ Cactus
☐ Camera
☐ Cowboy
☐ Dunce cap
☐ Elf
☐ Fisherman
☐ Flamingo
☐ Ghosts (2)
☐ Heart
☐ Ice-cream cones (2)
☐ Kite
☐ Old tire
☐ Picnic basket
☐ Quarter moon
☐ Robin Hood
☐ Sailor
☐ Santa Claus
☐ Skateboard
☐ Socks (2)
☐ Stepladder
☐ Telescope
☐ Tick-tack-toe
☐ Trash baskets (3)
☐ Turtle
☐ Witch

After the zoo, Frankie is a little hungry...

...so he goes to look for something to eat. He wonders if they serve his favorite monster mash here. Perhaps this would be a good place for the monsters to meet.

Before he gets lost again...

FIND FRANKIE AT THE YUM-YUM EMPORIUM AND...

☐ Arrow
☐ Birdcage
☐ Bone
☐ Chicken man
☐ Cook
☐ Dogs (3)
☐ Fishing pole
☐ Football
☐ Knight
☐ Mailbox
☐ Manager
☐ Panda
☐ Pirate
☐ Princess
☐ Robot
☐ Rubber duck
☐ Salt shaker
☐ Scuba diver
☐ Sheriff
☐ Skulls (2)
☐ Space creature
☐ Star
☐ Straws (2)
☐ Sunglasses (2)
☐ Tombstone
☐ Tray of pizza
☐ Tuba
☐ Turtles (2)
☐ Volcano
☐ Wig

After lunch, Frankie wanders into the aquarium to see some underwater monsters. Even though they're all wet, they seem to be having a good time.

FIND FRANKIE
IN THE AQUARIUM
AND...

☐ Boat
☐ Bucket
☐ Cans of tuna
☐ Cat
☐ Diver
☐ Dog
☐ Duck
☐ Ear
☐ Eyeglasses
☐ Fisherman
☐ Flying fish
☐ Guitar
☐ Hammer
☐ Hearts (4)
☐ Ice skater
☐ Igloo
☐ Life preserver
☐ Mermaid
☐ Magnifying glass
☐ Merman
☐ Old-fashioned radio
☐ Sea horse
☐ Socks (2)
☐ Starfish (3)
☐ Stingray
☐ Submarine
☐ Surfer
☐ Swordfish (2)
☐ Tick-tack-toe
☐ Tiger
☐ Water leak
☐ Wooden leg

After watching the fish frolic, Frankie feels like having some fun too.

Hot dog! It's Frankie's first time on wheels! If only his monster friends could see him now.

FIND FRANKIE AT THE ROWDY ROLLER RINK AND...

- ☐ Apple
- ☐ Artist
- ☐ Basketball
- ☐ Bowling ball
- ☐ Boxer
- ☐ Boy Scout
- ☐ Cave man
- ☐ Centaur
- ☐ Centipede
- ☐ Convict
- ☐ Drum
- ☐ Fire hydrant
- ☐ Fish
- ☐ Ghost
- ☐ Giant roller skate
- ☐ Guitar
- ☐ Half-stop sign
- ☐ Hockey player
- ☐ Ice skater
- ☐ Jugglers (2)
- ☐ Paintbrushes (2)
- ☐ Piano
- ☐ Pillow
- ☐ Scarfs (2)
- ☐ Skier
- ☐ Snow woman
- ☐ Super hero
- ☐ Swan
- ☐ Three-legged skater
- ☐ Unicorn
- ☐ Weight lifter
- ☐ Witch
- ☐ Zebra

After rocking and rolling around the rink, Frankie sees a place with lots of space monsters on video screens. He hears bloops and bleeps, bzaps and bliks—sounds that Frankie's friends usually make.

FIND FRANKIE IN THE ARCADE AND...

☐ Angel
☐ Baseball
☐ Bat
☐ Bathtub
☐ Bomb
☐ Bottle
☐ Bow
☐ Carrot
☐ Darts (4)
☐ Dog
☐ Earmuffs
☐ Giraffe
☐ Hammer
☐ Headless player
☐ Heart
☐ Highest score
☐ Horseshoe
☐ Ice-cream cone
☐ Jack-o'-lantern
☐ Painter
☐ Paper airplane
☐ Pillow
☐ Pinocchio
☐ Rabbit
☐ Robot
☐ Snakes (5)
☐ Spinning top
☐ Surfer
☐ Traffic ticket
☐ Trash can
☐ Wrecking ball

All the noise makes Frankie want to look for a peaceful place...

...outside of the city. This seems like a great place to live. If only he can find a nice, ugly home where the monsters can meet.

FIND FRANKIE IN THE SUBURBS AND...

- ☐ Badminton game
- ☐ Bird
- ☐ Caddy
- ☐ Candle
- ☐ Clown
- ☐ Cow
- ☐ Dogs (3)
- ☐ Duck
- ☐ Fencing star
- ☐ Fire hydrants (4)
- ☐ Flat tire
- ☐ Footballs (2)
- ☐ Hearts (3)
- ☐ Hose
- ☐ Hot dog mobile
- ☐ Ice-cream cone
- ☐ Ice skate
- ☐ Kite
- ☐ Lion
- ☐ Marching band
- ☐ Paper delivery
- ☐ Photographer
- ☐ Pig
- ☐ Pyramid
- ☐ Shark
- ☐ Telescope
- ☐ Treasure chest
- ☐ Tepee
- ☐ Umbrella
- ☐ Unicorn
- ☐ Unicycle
- ☐ Zebra

Wait! Maybe there is a place! Can you see it?

There, at the top of the hill, Frankie finds the perfect meeting house. The monsters finally find Frankie and elect him President of the Monster Club. What a great time for a party!

FIND FRANKIE AT THE MONSTERS' NEW CLUBHOUSE AND...

- ☐ Bats (4)
- ☐ Bones (4)
- ☐ Bottle
- ☐ Candles (2)
- ☐ Clock
- ☐ Coffeepot
- ☐ Coffin
- ☐ Cup
- ☐ Dog
- ☐ Flower
- ☐ Flying carpet
- ☐ Football
- ☐ Ghosts (5)
- ☐ Happy star
- ☐ Headless man
- ☐ Light bulb
- ☐ Mail carrier
- ☐ Mouse
- ☐ Mummy
- ☐ Octopus
- ☐ Pencil sharpener
- ☐ Skulls (4)
- ☐ Sled
- ☐ Snake
- ☐ Sword
- ☐ Tick-tack-toe
- ☐ Tombstones (2)
- ☐ Thirteens (4)
- ☐ Three-headed monster
- ☐ Top hat
- ☐ TV set
- ☐ Two-headed monster
- ☐ Umbrella
- ☐ Witch

FIND FRANKIE

SEARCH FOR SUSIE

LOOK FOR LAURA

DETECT DONALD

WHERE ARE THEY?

LOOK FOR LAURA

Laura lives on a planet called MAXX. One day she decided to visit her grandmother in her astro-ferry. All her friends came to say good-bye.

LOOK FOR LAURA ON THE PLANET MAXX AND...

- ☐ Balloons (3)
- ☐ Birdhouse
- ☐ Birds (2)
- ☐ Books (3)
- ☐ Clipboard
- ☐ Clocks (4)
- ☐ Coffeepot
- ☐ Covered wagon
- ☐ Dog
- ☐ Elephant
- ☐ Evergreen tree
- ☐ Fish
- ☐ Flowerpot
- ☐ Footballs (2)
- ☐ Fork
- ☐ Graduate
- ☐ Hamburger
- ☐ Hot dog
- ☐ Ice-cream pop
- ☐ Jump rope
- ☐ Kite
- ☐ Old radio
- ☐ Old tire
- ☐ Pizza
- ☐ Sled
- ☐ Tepee
- ☐ Train engine
- ☐ Turtle
- ☐ TV set
- ☐ Umbrella

But when Laura got into the astro-ferry, she pressed the wrong button.

Suddenly she was in an alien world surrounded by strange-looking creatures. Everything was wet! This wasn't her grandmother's house. This wasn't MAXX. This wasn't even land!

LOOK FOR LAURA IN THE OCEAN AND...

- ☐ Anchovy
- ☐ Bats (2)
- ☐ Bell
- ☐ Books (2)
- ☐ Bow
- ☐ Cheese
- ☐ Crown
- ☐ Cup
- ☐ Fire hydrant
- ☐ Flowers (2)
- ☐ Ghost
- ☐ Guitar
- ☐ Hammer
- ☐ Haystack
- ☐ Heart
- ☐ Horseshoe
- ☐ Ice-cream cone
- ☐ Key
- ☐ Mermaid
- ☐ Needlefish
- ☐ Octopus
- ☐ Old tire
- ☐ Pencil
- ☐ Pizza
- ☐ Saw
- ☐ Seesaw
- ☐ Snail
- ☐ Straw hat
- ☐ Telescope
- ☐ Treasure chest
- ☐ Turtles (3)
- ☐ TV set
- ☐ Umbrella

Laura zoomed up and finally landed...

...in a jungle watering hole. There the creatures were furry and feathery.

LOOK FOR LAURA AT THE WATERING HOLE AND...

- ☐ Arrow
- ☐ Balloons (3)
- ☐ Beach ball
- ☐ Birdbath
- ☐ Bird's nest
- ☐ Boat
- ☐ Bones (3)
- ☐ Camel
- ☐ Camera
- ☐ Crocodile
- ☐ Donkey
- ☐ Feather
- ☐ Football
- ☐ Giraffe
- ☐ Heart
- ☐ Jack-o'-lantern
- ☐ Joe of the jungle
- ☐ Lion
- ☐ Lollipop
- ☐ Owl
- ☐ Pelican
- ☐ Periscope
- ☐ Pig
- ☐ Rooster
- ☐ Snake
- ☐ Socks (2)
- ☐ Tin can
- ☐ Toucan
- ☐ Unicorn
- ☐ Wart hog
- ☐ Wolf
- ☐ Worm
- ☐ Yo-yo

But Laura wasn't sure if they were all friendly, so she got back on board and decided to explore the rest of this strange world.

As Laura flew through the sky, she saw some mountains covered with white stuff. Laura landed and for the very first time she saw— SNOW! This was fun! She wished her friends on MAXX could see the snow too.

LOOK FOR LAURA ON A SKI SLOPE IN THE ALPS AND...

☐ Alligator
☐ Artist
☐ Automobile
☐ Boat
☐ Bone
☐ Bunny
☐ Camel
☐ Cold telephone
☐ Dog
☐ Elf
☐ Evergreen tree
☐ Fish
☐ Football player
☐ Hammock
☐ Igloo
☐ Jack-o'-lantern
☐ Kite
☐ Mailbox
☐ Mouse
☐ Rake
☐ Santa Claus
☐ Scuba diver
☐ Skateboard
☐ Sleeping monster
☐ Snowman
☐ Sunglasses
☐ Top hat
☐ Turtle
☐ TV antenna
☐ Uphill skier

Then she was frightened by a loud yodel and away she went.

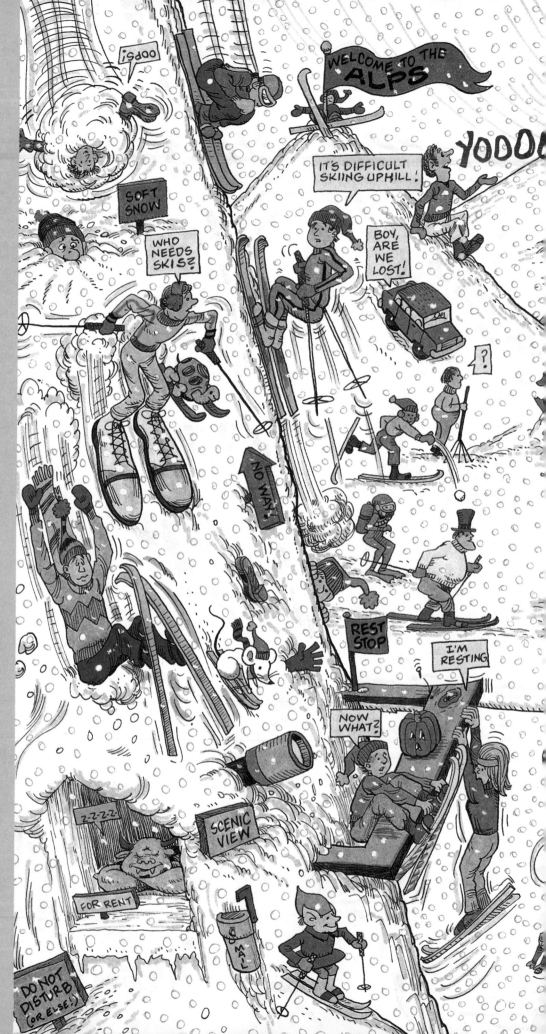

Laura flew south and landed in the desert—or rather, an oasis in the desert. Wow, it was hot! And people had towels on their heads! Everyone was too busy buying and selling at the bazaar to notice Laura, so she continued on her journey.

LOOK FOR LAURA AT THE BAH-HA BAZAAR AND...

☐ Beach ball
☐ Bird
☐ Broom
☐ Cat
☐ Clouds (2)
☐ Coconuts (4)
☐ Dog
☐ Donkey
☐ Elephant
☐ Flying carpets (2)
☐ Football
☐ Genie
☐ Horn
☐ Ice-cream cone
☐ Igloo
☐ Kite
☐ Necklace
☐ Oil well
☐ Pillow fight
☐ Rabbit
☐ Shovel
☐ Skier
☐ Sled
☐ Snail
☐ Snakes (4)
☐ Straw baskets (2)
☐ Sunglasses
☐ Telescope
☐ Tents (4)
☐ Truck
☐ Turtle
☐ Umbrella

Back north went the astro-ferry. Laura saw many beautiful places as she flew over Europe, so she decided to visit them.

LOOK FOR LAURA IN EUROPE AND...

- ☐ Automobiles (2)
- ☐ Ball
- ☐ Ballerinas (2)
- ☐ Boats (3)
- ☐ Cancan dancers
- ☐ Castle
- ☐ Dog
- ☐ Donkey
- ☐ Egret
- ☐ Fisherman
- ☐ Flying fish
- ☐ Ghost
- ☐ Gondola
- ☐ Hot-air balloon
- ☐ King
- ☐ Knight in armor
- ☐ Non-flying fish (3)
- ☐ Periscope
- ☐ Reindeer
- ☐ Skier
- ☐ Snake
- ☐ Snowmen (2)
- ☐ Starfish
- ☐ Stork
- ☐ Telescope
- ☐ Tour bus
- ☐ Train
- ☐ Tulips
- ☐ Turtle
- ☐ Windmill

Laura was beginning to get homesick and she wondered how she would find her way back to MAXX.

From the astro-ferry, Laura spotted a large group of children doing different activities. Maybe they could help.

LOOK FOR LAURA AT SUMMER CAMP AND...

☐ Alligator
☐ Basket
☐ Bats (2)
☐ Bear
☐ Broom
☐ Candy cane
☐ Cannon
☐ Cheese
☐ Cooks (2)
☐ Duck
☐ Firefighter
☐ Fish
☐ Head of a monster
☐ Headless monster
☐ Jack-o'-lantern
☐ Lake
☐ Lamp
☐ Motorcycle
☐ Owl
☐ Paper airplane
☐ Pizza
☐ Scarecrow
☐ Shovel
☐ Skateboard
☐ Skulls (2)
☐ Stepladder
☐ Target
☐ Telephone
☐ Three-legged chair
☐ Tin can
☐ Toy duck
☐ Wagon
☐ Witch

Laura had never seen so many strange activities. And no one had ever heard of the planet, MAXX.

The kids at camp directed Laura to a huge tent down the road. In the center of the tent, silly people, and animals too, seemed to be having fun.

LOOK FOR LAURA AT THE CIRCUS AND...

- ☐ Bad juggler
- ☐ Banana peel
- ☐ Binoculars
- ☐ Bowling ball
- ☐ Bow tie
- ☐ Cactus
- ☐ Cheese
- ☐ Cowboy hats (2)
- ☐ Dry paint
- ☐ Elephants (2)
- ☐ Ghost
- ☐ Hot dog
- ☐ Ice-cream cone
- ☐ Knight in armor
- ☐ Lion
- ☐ Lost shoe
- ☐ Monkey suit
- ☐ Mouse
- ☐ Picture frame
- ☐ Pie
- ☐ Pig
- ☐ Pirate
- ☐ Shoe shine box
- ☐ Skateboards (3)
- ☐ Top hat
- ☐ Training wheels
- ☐ Umbrella
- ☐ Walking flower
- ☐ Watering can

Laura enjoyed herself at the circus, but she was worried about getting home.

She tried again to get the astro-ferry to head for MAXX. Instead, she landed in a noisy city. Laura was about to give up hope of ever returning home. Then she saw some beings that looked a little like herself.

LOOK FOR LAURA IN WASHINGTON D.C. AND...

☐ Artist
☐ Birds (2)
☐ Bones (3)
☐ Books (3)
☐ Bows (4)
☐ Brush
☐ Camera
☐ Campaign poster
☐ Cat
☐ Envelope
☐ Goose
☐ Hammer
☐ Hard hats (2)
☐ Hot-air balloon
☐ Jogger
☐ Kangaroo
☐ Kite
☐ Magnifying glass
☐ Pentagon
☐ "People Working"
☐ Sailor's hat
☐ Scarecrow
☐ Secret agent
☐ Sleeping man
☐ Toolbox
☐ Turtle
☐ Tyrannosaurus
☐ Wagon
☐ Washington Monument

Perhaps they could help her, so she followed them as they walked...

...back to school! In the classroom, Laura watched the children do their spelling lessons. H-O-M-E spelled home.

LOOK FOR LAURA AT SCHOOL AND...

- ☐ Alexander
- ☐ Bat
- ☐ Bells (2)
- ☐ Broom
- ☐ Bubble gum
- ☐ Cat
- ☐ Clothespin
- ☐ Cupcake
- ☐ Drummer
- ☐ Easel
- ☐ Fish (2)
- ☐ Footballs (2)
- ☐ Globe
- ☐ Golf club
- ☐ Half moon
- ☐ Happy face
- ☐ Hats (2)
- ☐ Heart
- ☐ Hourglass
- ☐ Igloo
- ☐ Jump rope
- ☐ Monster mask
- ☐ Owl
- ☐ Paintbrush
- ☐ Pinocchio
- ☐ Plate
- ☐ Protoceratops
- ☐ Robin
- ☐ Robot
- ☐ School bags (2)
- ☐ Scissors
- ☐ Snow
- ☐ Soccer ball
- ☐ Stocking
- ☐ Sunglasses
- ☐ Wastepaper basket

Suddenly, Laura decided to type "M-A-X-X" in the astro-ferry's computer.

It worked! The astro-ferry zoomed home! Everyone was gathered to welcome her back to MAXX. Laura told them all about the many strange and wonderful things she had seen on Earth.

LOOK FOR LAURA AT THE WELCOME HOME PARTY AND...

- ☐ Alien-in-the-box
- ☐ Baseball cap
- ☐ Basket
- ☐ Bone
- ☐ Candle
- ☐ Carrot
- ☐ Cheese
- ☐ Cupcake
- ☐ Evergreen tree
- ☐ Falling stars (7)
- ☐ Fire hydrant
- ☐ Football
- ☐ Graduate
- ☐ Guitar
- ☐ Hamburger
- ☐ Hammer
- ☐ Hot dog
- ☐ Ice-cream soda
- ☐ Light bulb
- ☐ Meatball
- ☐ Mouse
- ☐ Pencils (2)
- ☐ Rose
- ☐ Screwdriver
- ☐ Shovel
- ☐ Snail
- ☐ Tent
- ☐ Turtle
- ☐ TV set
- ☐ Unicorn
- ☐ Yo-yo

From now on, Laura will be very careful when she travels in her astro-ferry.

DETECT DONALD   FIND FRANKIE   SEARCH FOR SUSIE   LOOK FOR LAURA

WHERE ARE THEY?

SEARCH FOR SUSIE

One day Susie's mom and dad took her to the Big Fun Amusement Park. Susie was excited and couldn't wait to see all the rides. While her parents were buying popcorn, Susie wandered off and started to explore the park.

SEARCH FOR SUSIE IN THE BIG FUN PARK AND...

☐ Banana peel
☐ Bowling ball
☐ Burst balloon
☐ Camel
☐ Candle
☐ Clothesline
☐ Clown-o-saurus (3)
☐ Ducks (2)
☐ Ear of corn
☐ Egg
☐ Football
☐ Ghost
☐ Hearts (2)
☐ Ice-cream cone
☐ Jack-o'-lantern
☐ Juggler
☐ Magnifying glass
☐ Megaphone
☐ Octopus
☐ Pencil
☐ Periscopes (2)
☐ Police (6)
☐ Raccoon
☐ Red wagon
☐ Reindeer
☐ Socks (2)
☐ Sour-puss-saurus
☐ Turtle
☐ Violinist

"Where's Susie?" asked her father.

"I don't know," answered her mother. "But we'd better start looking for her."

Meanwhile, Susie heard lots of shouting and splashing. Everyone seemed to be having fun. Or were they?

SEARCH FOR SUSIE AT THE WATER RIDE AND...

☐ Bone
☐ Bride
☐ Cactus
☐ Candy canes (2)
☐ Cupcake
☐ Curtains
☐ Dogs (2)
☐ Egg
☐ Fire hydrant
☐ Fish (4)
☐ Flying horse
☐ Goat
☐ Ground hog
☐ Hearts (3)
☐ Hobbyhorse
☐ Hot dog
☐ Island
☐ Moby Dick
☐ Nightmare
☐ Peter Pan
☐ Pickle barrel
☐ Police-o-saurus
☐ Sailboat
☐ Sea horse
☐ Surfboard
☐ Tuba
☐ Umbrella

Susie left the Water Ride
and headed for the
carousel. Around and
around it went. Susie
thought she heard her
parents calling her, but
with all the noise and
excitement she couldn't
find them.

SEARCH FOR
SUSIE AT THE
CAROUSEL AND...

☐ Alarm clock
☐ Ball
☐ Bat
☐ Broom
☐ Butterfly
☐ Cannon
☐ Dancing bears (2)
☐ Dentist
☐ Ear
☐ Fan
☐ Frog
☐ Golf bag
☐ Kangaroo
☐ Lamp
☐ Lollipop
☐ Mushroom
☐ Neckties (3)
☐ Parrot
☐ Pig
☐ Roller skate
☐ Scarecrow
☐ Snake
☐ Snow lady
☐ Super hero
☐ Telescope
☐ Top hat
☐ Truck
☐ Turtles (2)
☐ Unicorn
☐ Yo-yo

Susie's next stop was the Fun House. Wow! Things were really wild in there! Susie's mom and dad were searching for her in the Fun House too.

SEARCH FOR SUSIE IN THE FUN HOUSE AND...

- ☐ Banana peel
- ☐ Barrel
- ☐ Bib
- ☐ Cave man
- ☐ Cup
- ☐ Football helmet
- ☐ Headless body
- ☐ Humpty Dumpty
- ☐ Igloo
- ☐ Jack-in-a-box
- ☐ Jack-o'-lantern
- ☐ Kite
- ☐ Magician
- ☐ Medal
- ☐ Parachute
- ☐ Pie
- ☐ Pillow
- ☐ Pot
- ☐ Puppy
- ☐ Saw
- ☐ Sled
- ☐ Snake
- ☐ Sock
- ☐ Stool
- ☐ Susie's parents
- ☐ Target
- ☐ Traffic light
- ☐ Train engine
- ☐ Wacky clock
- ☐ Watermelon slice
- ☐ Wreath

Susie finally found her way through the maze and out of the Fun House. Then she heard loud, squeaking sounds which she followed to a huge, spinning Ferris wheel. "What a neat park this is," thought Susie.

SEARCH FOR SUSIE AT THE FERRIS WHEEL AND...

- ☐ Arrow
- ☐ Astronaut
- ☐ Birdhouse
- ☐ Broom
- ☐ Camera
- ☐ Candy cane
- ☐ Chimney
- ☐ Copycat
- ☐ Dinosaur guitarist
- ☐ Eye
- ☐ Golfer
- ☐ Hammock
- ☐ Hockey stick
- ☐ Ice skates
- ☐ Kite
- ☐ Lions (2)
- ☐ Oil can
- ☐ "Oup and Doup"
- ☐ Painters (2)
- ☐ Papa bear
- ☐ Plumber's plunger
- ☐ Santa Claus
- ☐ Screw
- ☐ Star
- ☐ Surfer
- ☐ Susie's parents
- ☐ Telephone
- ☐ Ticket collector
- ☐ Umbrella
- ☐ Watering can

Susie couldn't resist a ride on a roller coaster. Even an old, rickety-looking roller coaster. She bought a ticket and off she went!

SEARCH FOR SUSIE ON THE ROCK AND ROLLER COASTER RIDE AND...

☐ Balloons (5)
☐ Bat
☐ Birdcage
☐ Boat
☐ Can
☐ Carrot
☐ Cave man
☐ Dino-in-a-bottle
☐ Drummer
☐ Firefighter
☐ Fire hydrant
☐ Flames
☐ Flower eater
☐ Mailbox
☐ Moose
☐ Mummy
☐ Police-o-saurus
☐ Rabbits (5)
☐ Red tire
☐ Rocket
☐ Safe
☐ Skateboard
☐ Skier
☐ Sock
☐ Tennis racket
☐ Tick-tack-toe
☐ Unicycle
☐ Weights
☐ Window
☐ Wreath

Meanwhile, Susie's parents were still searching for her.

After a thrilling ride on the roller coaster, Susie needed a nice, quiet place to relax. The Game Room seemed like the perfect spot. Not much was happening there.

SEARCH FOR SUSIE IN THE GAME ROOM AND...

☐ Apples (2)
☐ Baseball
☐ Basketball
☐ Bomb
☐ Boomerang
☐ Can
☐ Candle
☐ Carrot
☐ Coffeepot
☐ Cup
☐ Dice
☐ Donkey's tail
☐ Dracula
☐ Earmuffs
☐ Ghost
☐ Gift box
☐ Graduate
☐ Guitar
☐ Hammer
☐ Horseshoe
☐ Pencil
☐ Poodle
☐ Sailboat
☐ Telescope
☐ Timekeeper
☐ Top hat
☐ Turtles (3)
☐ Umpire
☐ Unicorn
☐ Yo-yo

Susie played a few games, then headed for...

...the bumper cars! What an exciting ride that was! Susie banged and bumped and crashed her way from one end to the other. She waved to her parents who unfortunately got bumped before they could see her.

SEARCH FOR SUSIE ON THE BUMPER CARS AND...

- ☐ Alien
- ☐ Artist
- ☐ Banana peel
- ☐ Birdcage
- ☐ Bride
- ☐ Cactus
- ☐ Camel
- ☐ Candy cane
- ☐ Cans (5)
- ☐ Car "007"
- ☐ Car "8A"
- ☐ Car "54"
- ☐ Cat
- ☐ Crown
- ☐ Fire hydrant
- ☐ Giraffes (2)
- ☐ Hot dog
- ☐ Ice-cream cone
- ☐ Jack-o'-lantern
- ☐ Kite
- ☐ Light bulb
- ☐ Mice (2)
- ☐ Musician
- ☐ Pig
- ☐ Police (2)
- ☐ Shoemobile
- ☐ Speed limit
- ☐ Stars (2)
- ☐ Sunglasses
- ☐ Surfer
- ☐ Target

After a long day of fun, Susie was getting hungry. She wondered where she might find a delicious banana split. Then Susie spotted a giant ice-cream cone.

SEARCH FOR SUSIE AT THE ICE-CREAM SHOP AND...

- ☐ Bad-news lizard
- ☐ Balloons (3)
- ☐ Clock
- ☐ Drum
- ☐ Eyeglasses
- ☐ Fish
- ☐ Fudge pop
- ☐ Igloo
- ☐ Kangaroo
- ☐ King Kong
- ☐ Mushroom
- ☐ Paint bucket
- ☐ Santa Claus
- ☐ Sled
- ☐ Slice of pie
- ☐ Snail
- ☐ Socks (2)
- ☐ Sombrero
- ☐ Spoon
- ☐ Teeth
- ☐ Telescope
- ☐ Tepee
- ☐ Tire
- ☐ Top hat
- ☐ Toy duck
- ☐ Toy train
- ☐ TV set
- ☐ Umbrella
- ☐ Unicorn

Mom and Dad were still searching and searching for Susie. And...

...there she was! On the giant swings! Susie couldn't wait to tell them about all the fun she had in the Big Fun Amusement Park.

SEARCH FOR SUSIE ON THE GIANT SWINGS AND...

☐ Bat
☐ Bell
☐ Birdhouse
☐ Blue sneaker
☐ Bone
☐ Broken ropes (3)
☐ Broom
☐ Bucket of red paint
☐ Candle
☐ Car
☐ Carrot
☐ Chickens (2)
☐ Fish
☐ Football
☐ Fork
☐ Genie
☐ Horn
☐ Human acrobats (2)
☐ Ice-cream cone
☐ Ice skate
☐ Magnifying glass
☐ Paper airplane
☐ Parachute
☐ Scissors
☐ Slingshot
☐ Snake
☐ Soccer ball
☐ Stars (4)
☐ Ticket collector
☐ Top hat
☐ Waiter
☐ Wrecking ball

SEARCH FOR SUSIE   LOOK FOR LAURA   DETECT DONALD   FIND FRANKIE

APR 0 1 2013

El Dorado Hills Branch